STUMP YOUR
LAWYER!

STUMP YOUR LAWYER!

A QUIZ TO CHALLENGE
THE LEGAL MIND

HOWARD ZAHAROFF

CHRONICLE BOOKS
SAN FRANCISCO

Copyright © 2007 Howard G. Zaharoff.

Library of Congress Cataloging-in-Publication Data:

Zaharoff, Howard G.

Stump your lawyer! : a quiz to challenge the legal mind / by Howard Zaharoff.

p. cm.

ISBN-13: 978-0-8118-5820-5

ISBN-10: 0-8118-5820-0

1. Law—United States—Miscellanea. 2. Law—United States—Humor. I. Title.

KF387.Z34 2007

349.73—dc22

2006100256

Manufactured in Canada

Designed by Alice Chau

Cover design by Alice Chau

The images at questions 12, 45, 90, 164, and 195 are from The Library of Congress, Prints & Photographs Division, reproduction numbers LC-USZC62-60141, LC-USZ62-86846, LC-DIG-cwph-05620 (digital file from LC-B8172-1747), LC-USZ62-52153 (copy of engraving by Alexander Hay Ritchie), and LC-USZ61-1761. The image at question 133 is from The Boston Herald (1920).

Distributed in Canada by Raincoast Books

9050 Shaughnessy Street

Vancouver, British Columbia V6P 6E5

10 9 8 7 6 5 4 3 2 1

Chronicle Books LLC

680 Second Street

San Francisco, California 94107

www.chroniclebooks.com

To Josh, Marta, and Leah, who time and again remind me of the joys of new challenges.

To my parents, Artie and Dottie, and my mother-in-law, Rosalie, who daily prove that youth is just an attitude.

And to my wife, Debbie, who has not only encouraged, cajoled, and challenged me to do and be the best I can, but has also tolerated my sense of humor for over three decades.

Special thanks to several people who have helped make this book possible, and better: Jay Schaefer, my "your contract is in the mail" editor and inspiration[1]; Jim Grace, one of the most graceful and generous lawyers I know; Jim Corrigan, a talented writer, humorist, and breakfast buddy, who improved more answers than I can shake a writ at; my son Josh, who added humor and spared readers some relentless minutiae (though there's plenty left); and my friends Bob Dushman, Ron Fellman, and Ellen Kozak, each of whom helped enormously. Though I suspect that readers of this book will question several answers and analyses, if that number is low, it's because these lawyers were on their toes.

Also, a special thanks to Dr. Steve Birnbaum for the photograph at question 37. That photo is ©2007 Steven Birnbaum.

Of course, I still take full credit for any errors or faulty logic you uncover. Isn't that what it means to be a lawyer in 21st-century America?

---

[1] He also kept me from titling this book *How to Grill a Lawyer** (**This Is a Test, Not a Cookbook*). If any of you prefer this title, please drop him a line. He'll love to hear from you.

It's inevitable that sometime, somewhere, you'll need a lawyer.

Think about it. The law surrounds us like a seamless web. Not only does it control our lives from birth to death, but it also affects us before we're born (e.g., alcohol-labeling laws) and well after we're laid to rest (e.g., inheritance laws and cemetery regulations).

So, whether you're leasing an apartment, probating your great-aunt's estate, negotiating a dry-cleaning ticket, dealing with your teenager's DUI arrest, unleashing a pit bull, or doing any of a million other things ordinary Americans do regularly, at some point you'll need the help of a good lawyer.

But how do you find one? Or, more to the point, how do you know you've found a good one?

By proper application of the questions that follow, you will be able to use this book to determine with nearly 100 percent accuracy[2] whether the lawyer you'd like to hire is top-notch legal talent.[3]

What *is* top-notch legal talent? In a nutshell, the ideal lawyer needs street smarts, a command of facts, a knowledge of law, the ability to reason, a mastery of legal mumbo jumbo, and the skill to withstand tough questioning—from you.

---

[2] FEDERAL TRADE COMMISSION COMPLIANCE NOTICE: No research or studies whatsoever have been conducted to confirm the accuracy of this statement. We didn't even spell-check.

[3] If not, we suggest you leave them your copy of this book—they probably need it more than you do—and promptly buy yourself a fresh copy before your next interview.

This book can measure brainpower, knowledge, and reasoning skill, and you can rule out lawyers who can't answer most of the questions that follow. But how can a book of questions and answers—no matter how scintillating, insightful, and just plain hilarious—measure the instinct to go for the kill that is the *sine qua non* of the zealous advocate?

It's easy. Many lawyers, intimidated or merely polite, will answer questions, nod solemnly, and let you proceed to the next question. Such lawyers might be suitable if you are seeking someone to draft your will or teach civil procedure to first-year law students. But even if they are correct in all their responses, these are *less-than-ideal lawyers*, the type that won't jump from their chairs every five seconds to object to a question by opposing counsel.

Other lawyers will scornfully answer a few questions and then leap up, grab the book from your hands, toss it across the room, and exclaim that the book's a sham, the author's a fool, and you're an idiot.

Eureka! Such a display of arrogance and aggression tells you *this person is worth hiring*. Does the candidate really know what's what and resent being quizzed, or did this target have a few lucky guesses and is now bluffing his or her way out? It doesn't matter, since *how a lawyer handles these questions is as important as the answers themselves*.

Note to lawyers: This book is for you, too. Unless you do *every-thing* well, which is not likely, at some point you'll need to find a lawyer to represent you. (Though, as the saying goes, a lawyer who represents himself as a client is far less likely to overcharge for meal expenses, unless they're deductible.) And until that happens, you might want to practice up on some of these questions. So treat this book as a bar-review refresher course for the day when a consumer-savvy potential client comes through the door to see what *you* know.

Note for everyone: To enhance the readability of this book, the author has taken several liberties.

First, nothing in the law is black-and-white, and every legal rule, principle, and holding has exceptions. Therefore, to avoid peppering every answer that follows with qualifiers such as "likely," "probably," and "usually" (for example, I was dying to write that "practically nothing is black-and-white"), I have used these terms only when the answer is truly close or hard to call.

Second, following the same principle, to avoid boringly repeating words such as "about," "around," and "approximately," and phrases like "it is estimated," I just state the damn number.

Finally, good lawyers know that anyone can sue anyone else for anything anywhere anytime. Still, to keep things snappy, I use *sue* as shorthand for more accurate but clunkier phrases like "could sue successfully," "has a bona fide legal claim," and "has substantial grounds for a lawsuit."

Please recall these comments as you read the answers that follow, and do not think ill of the author, editors, or publisher for the use of unqualified and straightforward language. (We also wanted to give ourselves wiggle room.)

LEGAL DISCLAIMER NO. 1: This book is not legal advice. You want legal advice, hire a lawyer.

LEGAL DISCLAIMER NO. 2: This book does not establish a lawyer-client relationship between the author and the reader, and it is not intended to be relied upon in analyzing legal claims. Actually, in many states it would be considered advertising, and you wouldn't rely on advertising for legal advice, would you? Only by properly engaging a lawyer and agreeing to pay his or her sticker-shock hourly rate, plus reimbursement for long-distance phone calls, short-distance phone calls, intermediate-range phone calls, conference calls, conference room usage, document reproduction, document storage, document shredding, telefax, courier, messenger service, after-hours meals charges, and late-night cab fare do you earn the right to enter into a lawyer-client relationship and then sue that person for the least mistake.

LEGAL DISCLAIMER NO. 3: The lawyer who wrote this book has been disbarred in three states. He went to an unaccredited law school and fakes credentials in official documents and on book jackets. Warning! Warning! *Under no circumstances should you rely on his words.*

1 Which states have laws that limit ballpark owners' liability to fans hit by foul balls?

(A) None of them

(B) All of them

(C) Massachusetts, New York, and Texas

(D) Arizona, Colorado, Illinois, and New Jersey

2 True or False?

If advertisements for a new movie state, "Critics agree this is the Must-See Action Film of the summer," and in fact the critics do not agree this is the Must-See Action Film of the summer, or any other season, you can recover the ticket price if you really hate the film.

3 Hypothetical:

A giant gorilla, brought to New York by Jack, an entertainment magnate, escapes from a show and, after wreaking havoc—including destroying Naomi's car—climbs to the top of the Empire State Building, where Air Force fighter planes shoot him down. When the ape falls, he crushes Adrien's car, which is parked on the street below. Can Naomi or Adrien recover for their misfortunes?

4 Article I of the U.S. Constitution

(A) Describes the people's desire "to form a more perfect Union"

(B) Describes the power and qualifications of the President

(C) Describes the powers and composition of Congress

(D) Contains the table of contents for Articles II, III, and IV

1   (D)

2 False (The ad is puffery that no reasonable moviegoer would take seriously.)

3 It's doubtful either can sue the government, but if they have collision insurance, they can get their cars repaired, or payment in lieu of repair.

Naomi has a strict liability claim against Jack for damage caused by his wild animal. Also, unless he received approval from the New York City Department of Health, Jack violated the NYC Health Code by keeping and exhibiting the primate. Even with approval, he breached the code by using inadequate measures to prevent the ape's escape.

Adrien's claim is weak: damage caused by a machine-gunned ape's fall from a tall building seems too remote a possibility. Still, given Jack's overall misconduct, a suit is worth a try.

Should Adrien sue the Empire State Building's builder or owner for negligently failing to put a high parapet around the roof? Probably not.

4 (C)

5 **The first words of the U.S. Constitution are**

(A) "Fourscore and seven years ago..."

(B) "We the People of the United States..."

(C) "These are the times that try men's souls."

(D) "It was a dark and stormy night."

6 **To what does the term "Hammurabi" refer?**

(A) A hooded executioner in India

(B) The giver of the first code of laws

(C) A type of sushi

(D) Honda's first hybrid vehicle

7 **U.S. Supreme Court Justice Byron White was given the nickname "Whizzer" because**

(A) He won many math awards in high school

(B) He was an All-American running back in college

(C) He had a hyperactive bladder

(D) None of the above—his real nickname was "Satchmo"

8 **The Treaty of Rome**

(A) Divided Gaul into three parts

(B) Established the Italian Soccer League

(C) Ensured that all roads do, in fact, lead there

(D) Created the European Union

5 Ⓑ

6 Ⓑ

7 Ⓑ

8 Ⓓ

9 What important work begins, "When in the Course of human events..."?

(A) The Declaration of Independence

(B) The National Anthem

(C) The Bill of Rights

(D) *Death to Smoochy*

10 Hypothetical:

Jane asks a friend whether she can borrow his car but doesn't tell him she needs it for a job interview. The friend agrees, but when Jane goes to get the car, the friend says he changed his mind. Jane pleads, but the friend is unmoved. Jane misses the interview and loses the job.

A Can Jane sue for breach of contract?

B Would it make a difference if she told her friend she needed the car for a job interview?

C Would it make a difference if, a week later, Jane received a letter from the interviewer saying it's too bad she missed the interview, since on the basis of her résumé, he was going to offer her a job on the spot for $125,000 per year?

11 The Alien and Sedition Acts, enabling the federal government to quell opposition and punish treason, were enacted under which President?

(A) John Adams

(B) John Quincy Adams

(C) George H. W. Bush

(D) George W. Bush

9

10 (A) No breach of contract because there was no contract. The friend's offer was a favor, not a bargained-for commitment.

(B) Yes, stating why she needed the car should make a difference. Although there was still no contract, Jane relied on the friend to her detriment, and he knew that. But it may be hard to prove damages, since no one knows whether she would have gotten the job.

(C) Yes, receiving the letter makes a difference, since the letter lets Jane show specific, non-speculative injury.

11

12 The following is a picture of whom?

(A) Buddy Holly, singer

(B) Leatherface, from *The Texas Chainsaw Massacre*

(C) William Kunstler, defense lawyer

(D) William Rehnquist, former Chief Justice of the Supreme Court

13 To die intestate means to die

(A) From a perforated intestine or testicle

(B) Subject to the jurisdiction of two or more states

(C) Without a will

(D) Literally "untested"; thus, without a spouse or children

14 Which of the following cannot be protected as a trademark in the U.S.?

(A) The scent of yarn

(B) The color of fiberglass insulation

(C) The sound of a Harley-Davidson engine

(D) The shape of a Coke bottle

(E) All of the above are disqualified

15 Who said, "Fifty percent of the job of a good lawyer is to tell the client he's a damn fool and should stop"?

(A) Elihu Root

(B) Abraham Lincoln

(C) John Dean

(D) Raymond Burr

QUESTIONS

12 D

13 C

14 C (The Harley-Davidson sound is purely functional and therefore unprotectable.)

15 A

16 The "doctrine of equivalents" is used to

(A) Establish that something falling outside the literal scope of a patent is similar enough to infringe

(B) Prove that schools are "separate but equal" under the 14th Amendment

(C) Compare damage calculations in tort law

(D) Justify the sale of Babe Ruth to the Yankees in 1919

17 Hypothetical:

Don owns a small business, organized as an S corporation, which needs capital to grow. Robert, recently returned from Moscow, has several Russian friends who want to invest in an American company. He tells Don that he can raise money, but he wants a 5 percent finder's fee. Using Robert's help in negotiations, Don sells these Russians 25 percent of his company for $500,000 and pays Robert $25,000. Any concerns?

18 Who originally took an oath "to protect and defend the Constitution...and to protect the States and the people thereof from all invasion from any source whatsoever"?

(A) The President of the United States

(B) Navy ROTC cadets

(C) Boy Scouts

(D) Knights of the Ku Klux Klan

19 Who vows to keep "physically strong, mentally awake, and morally straight"?

(A) Navy ROTC cadets

(B) Boy Scouts

(C) Disney World employees

(D) Teenage Mutant Ninja Turtles

16

17 Foreign ownership will cancel Don's S election—he's
now a C corporation, subject to two levels of tax. Also,
since Robert appears not to be a registered broker-dealer,
his being paid to raise capital violates federal and state
securities laws. He could be sued by the Securities and Exchange Commission and state authorities and may owe the
Russians their money back. The company itself may have
violated securities laws and may be at risk of rescission.

18

19

20 The process by which the state takes private property without the owner's consent is called

(A) Eminence grise

(B) Eminent domain

(C) Gerrymandering

(D) Robbing Peter to pay Paul

21 Obtaining title to another person's property by open and hostile use is known as

(A) Finders keepers

(B) Losers weepers

(C) Homesteading

(D) Adverse possession

22 Hypothetical:

Phyllis decides to build a trellis in her backyard but inadvertently builds it on her neighbor's land. Two years later, the neighbor sells his property to Joel, whose survey discloses the mistake. Joel tells Phyllis she needs to move her trellis back to her own property line. Phyllis refuses, arguing that it's only two useless feet of dirt and that the move would kill her vines. Twelve years later, Phyllis sells her property to Mark, telling him about the trellis. Despite Joel's request, Mark also refuses to move the trellis. This continues for five more years.

A Who owns the disputed land?

B Is the situation any different four years later?

20 Ⓑ (and sometimes Ⓓ)

21 Ⓓ

22 Ⓐ Joel still owns the land (though some states would recognize Phyllis's and Mark's claims if they paid taxes on the disputed turf).

Ⓑ Four years later, after more than twenty years of "open and hostile" possession, most jurisdictions would recognize Mark as the owner by "tacking" (adding) his adverse-possession claim onto Phyllis's. (Some states, such as Iowa and Georgia, require "innocent" possession, while others require tax payments, so the outcome varies by state.)

23 Technically, to "impeach" a government official is to

(A) Try the official by a jury of pears

(B) Try the official for a crime

(C) Accuse the official of a crime

(D) Convict the official of a crime

24 Article I.8.11 of the U.S. Constitution gives Congress the power to grant "letters of marque." What can recipients of such letters do?

(A) Coin money

(B) Operate a post road

(C) Seize enemy vessels

(D) Grant titles such as marquis

25 The principle that people should not be found guilty of a crime if, due to mental defect, they cannot distinguish right from wrong is known as

(A) The Durham Rule

(B) The M'Naghten Rule

(C) The Peter Principle

(D) The Clinton Principle

26 The following portrait depicts whom?

(A) Daniel M'Naghten, source of the M'Naghten insanity rule

(B) John Jay, first Chief Justice of the U.S. Supreme Court

(C) Hammurabi, Giver of Laws

(D) Martha Washington, wife of the first President

23 Ⓒ

24 Ⓒ

25 Ⓑ

26 Ⓑ

27 Which states do not allow an insanity defense?

(A) Idaho, Montana, and Utah

(B) California, Florida, and Hawaii

(C) The Red States

(D) None—all states recognize this defense

28 What percentage of defendants pleads not guilty by reason of insanity?

(A) 1%

(B) 5%

(C) 10%

(D) 25%

29 What percentage of insanity pleas is successful?

(A) 1%

(B) 5%

(C) 10%

(D) 25%

30 One of the first prominent uses of the insanity defense in the United States occurred when politician and Civil War hero Dan Sickles was tried for killing his wife's lover. The lover was the son of whom?

(A) George Washington

(B) Aaron Burr

(C) Francis Scott Key

(D) Tom Paine

31 When South Carolina seceded from the Union, precipitating the Civil War, anti-secessionist James Petigru described his state as "too small to be a nation and too large to be _____."

27 Ⓐ

28 Ⓐ

29 Ⓓ

30   (The elder Key wrote "The Star-Spangled Banner.")

31 "An insane asylum"

32 **Hypothetical:**

John undergoes complex forearm-lengthening surgery under general anesthesia. He wakes up with severe neck pain and is out of work for weeks. The hospital denies liability, arguing there is no proof the medical staff did anything wrong. John's lawyer produces an expert who says that it is highly unusual for someone to experience such injuries from forearm surgery that's done properly. The lawyer argues that, therefore, this unexplained injury is itself sufficient to show negligence.

What is that argument called?

(A) *Illigitimi non carborundum*

(B) *Res ipsa loquitur*

(C) *Gallia divisa in partes tres*

(D) Long arm jurisdiction

More importantly, is John likely to win under these facts? Would it matter if he had a history of neck problems not known to the medical staff?

33 Wisconsin law prohibits any building in Madison from being higher than

(A) The Robert LaFollette Tower

(B) The Racine Holiday Inn

(C) The Capitol Building

(D) The Cheese Curd Memorial

34 How many states allow marriage between first cousins?

(A) 50

(B) 26

(C) 12

(D) 0

32 The argument is called *res ipsa loquitur*, "the thing speaks for itself," and, yes, John should win. In fact, even if John had neck problems, unless the hospital can prove these caused the injury, he should still win, since the circumstances suggest the staff just wasn't careful enough.

Note: If the hospital's lawyer had given John a good consent form to sign, things might have turned out differently.

33

34 Ⓑ (plus Washington, D.C., although several impose conditions, such as being age 65 or older.)

35 Third cousins are people who share

(A) Great-grandparents

(B) Great-great-grandparents

(C) Great-great-great grandparents

(D) 99.8% identical DNA (but only 84.5% of the time)

(E) A high number of annoying second cousins once removed

36 Hypothetical:

Monica asks her friend Hillary to bring her favorite dress—worn, but in fine condition—to the XYZ Cleaners to remove a stain. Hillary brings it instead to the nearby ABC Cleaners. The ticket ABC gives Hillary has a prominent disclaimer stating that ABC isn't responsible for damage. When Monica goes to retrieve the dress, she discovers a large hole where the stain used to be. When Monica points this out to the ABC clerk and says she wants ABC to pay for a new dress, the clerk cites the disclaimer but offers to have one of ABC's workers stitch up the hole. The clerk admits the repair will be noticed, but argues it is a great offer, since their ticket shields them from liability. How great an offer is it? Does Monica have any claim against Hillary?

37 A New Hampshire photographer claims this is Mick Jagger in concert. If used in this book without anyone's consent, which statement would be correct?

(A) This use violates Jagger's publicity rights and the photographer's copyright

(B) This use violates Jagger's rights but is a copyright fair use

(C) This use violates the photographer's copyright but not Jagger's rights

(D) This use violates no one's rights

(35)

(36) Monica can't sue her friend. Though most courts would ignore the cleaner's liability disclaimer, many would find a repair sufficient. Others might also allow Monica to recover the difference in value between the repaired dress and the undamaged dress—probably not much, since the dress was already used.

(37) That the use is editorial, educational, and equivocal avoids violating Jagger's rights—or so the publisher hopes. Ordinarily, using a photo in this manner would not be a fair use. Oddly, however, using the photo to illustrate the concept of a use that is not a fair use may, with complete circularity, make the use a fair use and thus make the correct answer (D). Still, to be safe, we got the photographer's permission.

38 **True or False?**

If a teen's first offense is possession of one joint of marijuana, in Massachusetts the teen will be put on probation, but in Nevada the youth risks four years in prison and a $5,000 fine.

39 **The language "hereby remises and forever discharges, from all claims, demands, and liabilities whatsoever, from the beginning of the world to this date" is found in**

(A) A will

(B) A mortgage

(C) A settlement agreement

(D) The Book of Genesis

40 **Who said, "A lawyer's time and advice are his stock in trade"?**

(A) Clarence Darrow

(B) Clarence Thomas

(C) Abraham Lincoln

(D) Yogi Berra

41 **A trial lawyer in the United Kingdom is known as a**

(A) Solicitor

(B) Barrister

(C) Strumpet

(D) Bandersnatch

42 **The Bayh-Dole Act regulates which of the following?**

(A) Banking industries

(B) Pineapple growers

(C) Free speech

(D) Technology commercialization

38   True.

39   Ⓒ

40   Ⓒ

41   Ⓑ

42. Ⓓ

43 The Magnusson-Moss Act regulates which of the following?

- (A) Iron levels in drinking water
- (B) Patent protection for plants
- (C) Consumer warranties
- (D) Sitcom laugh tracks

44 If a friend leaves me "in loco parentis," she has left me

- (A) Crazy about parentheses
- (B) Obliged to pay her rent
- (C) With a small part in a local theater production
- (D) In charge of her children

45 This is a photograph of whom?

- (A) Sandra Dee O'Connor
- (B) Sandra Day O'Connor
- (C) Sinead Day O'Connor
- (D) One of the Olsen twins

46 Hypothetical:

Jill, a Massachusetts resident, buys a digital camera from a Web site run by a small business in New Mexico. The camera arrives damaged, but the site disclaims responsibility, arguing that (1) the damage occurred in transit and (2) according to its terms of use (accessible by a tiny link at the bottom of the home page), the site isn't responsible for such losses. The terms also state that disputes must be arbitrated in New Mexico. Since there was no click-through process on the site, however, Jill wasn't aware of these terms. Does she have a claim against the site? Can she bring suit in court, or must she arbitrate? Can she bring her claim in Massachusetts, or must she prosecute in New Mexico?

43 Ⓒ

44 Ⓓ

45 Ⓑ

46 Jill can sue the Web site in court, because these terms don't create a contract. She can sue in Massachusetts, unless this was an isolated sale and the defendant neither conducted nor targeted other Massachusetts business.

47 Under federal food-labeling guidelines, to be called "fat free" a product must have

(A) No fat

(B) Less than .1 gram per referenced amount and, as to ingredients with fat, a footnote warning: "We have hidden significant fat in fatty ingredients; contact Ingredient Manufacturer for details."

(C) Less than .5 gram per referenced amount and serving and, as to ingredients with fat, an asterisked notice such as "Adds a trivial amount of fat."

(D) Less than 5 grams per referenced amount and serving and, as to ingredients with fat, a notice: "There may be more fat here than meets the eye; for details, contact our Vice President for Fat Content."

48 If a product gets less than half its calories from fat, to be described as "light," it must have

(A) ⅔ fewer calories than the referenced amount

(B) ½ less fat or ⅓ fewer calories than the referenced amount

(C) ⅔ less fat and ⁴¹⁄₇₅ fewer calories than the referenced amount

(D) An amount of fat that the manufacturer, in its reasonable judgment, believes the average consumer would be pleased to call "light."

49 In 2004, Massachusetts became the first state (though it calls itself a "Commonwealth") to allow couples of the same sex to

(A) Vote

(B) Adopt

(C) Breakdance

(D) Marry

47 Ⓒ

48 Ⓑ

49 Ⓓ

50 What states, in addition to Massachusetts, refer to themselves as a "Commonwealth"?

51 The ruling of the Massachusetts Supreme Judicial Court that permits gay marriage was based on the Court's interpretation of

(A) The U.S. Constitution

(B) The Massachusetts Constitution

(C) The City of Cambridge Constitution

(D) *La Cage Aux Folles*

52 Under Massachusetts law, gift certificates must be good for at least

(A) 2 years

(B) 4 years

(C) 7 years

(D) Indefinitely

53 Under California law, gift certificates must be good for at least

(A) 2 years

(B) 4 years

(C) 7 years

(D) Indefinitely

50 Pennsylvania, Virginia, and Kentucky

51 Ⓑ

52 Ⓒ

53 Ⓓ

54 New York City anti-scalping laws permit ticket holders to sell event tickets

(A) For face value only

(B) For face value plus 10%

(C) For up to the premium price printed on the ticket

(D) Back to the event sponsor only

55 Under the 1982 U.N. Convention on the Law of the Sea, every coastal nation can establish its territorial sea as long as it doesn't exceed

(A) 10 miles

(B) 50 miles

(C) 12 nautical miles

(D) 100 nautical miles

56 A nautical mile, by international agreement, is

(A) The same length as a regular mile, but headed straight down

(B) Twice the length of a regular mile, but only half the width

(C) 15% longer than a regular mile

(D) The distance a boat moving at 60 knots travels in 10 minutes

57 In 2001, the U.S. and the European Union resolved a dispute concerning the E.U.'s rules on the importation of

(A) Military weaponry

(B) Wide-body jets

(C) Motion pictures

(D) Bananas

54 Ⓒ (but ticket brokers can mark up by 10%)

55 Ⓒ

56 Ⓒ

57 Ⓓ

58 Hypothetical:

A musician composes and records a song but doesn't get a record deal. Two years later she is paid $150 to assign all rights to her song and performance in writing. Five years later she dies. Five years after her death the recording is included in a CD that sells well. The musician's heirs can reclaim her copyright in the song

(A) Immediately

(B) In 15 years (a copyright can be reclaimed 20 years after the artist's death)

(C) In 25 years (a copyright can be reclaimed 35 years after its transfer)

(D) Never

59 After being pulled over in your car by a police officer, the first thing you should do is

(A) Rummage through your glove box to find your registration

(B) Stash your weed under your seat

(C) Offer the officer a doughnut

(D) Stay seated and roll down your window

60 Trademarks can have real value; the estimated value of the Coca-Cola brand is

(A) $70 million

(B) $700 million

(C) $70 billion

(D) $7 bazillion

58 Ⓒ

59 Ⓓ

60 Ⓒ

61 Which of the following is *not* among the world's 20 most valuable trademarks?

(A) Lego

(B) Marlboro

(C) GE

(D) Nokia

62 "Cy pres" refers to

(A) Appointment of a temporary CEO

(B) Award for the best pitchers in Major League Baseball

(C) Court order to refurnish in hardwood

(D) Court enforcing terms of will or trust as closely as possible

63 The Sherman Antitrust Act concerns

(A) Post–Civil War statute banning Union troops from Georgia

(B) Monopolization of market power

(C) Price discrimination in interstate commerce

(D) Cruel betrayal of Charlie Brown by his closest friends

64 The average American business loses what percentage of revenues to fraud?

(A) 1%

(B) 6%

(C) 10%

(D) 22%

61 Ⓐ

62 Ⓓ

63 Ⓑ

64 Ⓑ

65 A "holographic" will is

(A) Incomplete, thus only partly enforceable

(B) Created out of holograms

(C) Written by hand

(D) A will in which the testator and the beneficiary are of the same sex

66 A "nuncupative" will is

(A) An oral will

(B) A bequest by a member of a religious order

(C) A will devising property the testator doesn't own

(D) A will rendered unenforceable by a subsequent will

67 Which of the following actors played a lawyer who wins his case?

(A) Gregory Peck in *To Kill a Mockingbird*

(B) Joe Pesci in *My Cousin Vinny*

(C) Spencer Tracy in *Inherit the Wind*

(D) Kevin Bacon in *A Few Good Men*

65 Ⓒ

66 Ⓐ

67 Ⓑ

68 **Hypothetical:**

For her birthday Shania, a singer, asks an assistant to get her the lyrics to Roy Orbison's "Oh Pretty Woman." The assistant buys a book of Orbison's greatest hits, then makes fifty photocopies of the lyrics to give the singer and her party guests. Before thirty friends and family, Shania belts out the song. A friend asks her to perform it again for a benefit she is running for a local environmental-advocacy group, which Shania does. The concert is organized by unpaid volunteers, and the admission fee is used entirely for overhead and charitable purposes. No one asks for permission to copy or perform the song. Does Shania or her friend have a problem? What if the Orbison estate learns of the concert and, six days in advance, sends a letter objecting to the unlicensed use of the song in a concert where admission is charged?

69 **After the 2004 Presidential election, JibJab Media was threatened with a copyright suit for creating an online animation parody of the Bush and Kerry campaigns using what song?**

(A) "Yellow Rose of Texas"

(B) "This Land is Your Land"

(C) "Don't Stop (Thinking About Tomorrow)"

(D) "It's Hard Out Here for a Pimp"

70 **In which state do bingo volunteers have limited immunity if they injure someone during play?**

(A) California

(B) Florida

(C) Texas

(D) Illinois

68 Shania's private performance is fine, but her assistant's fifty copies infringe. The group's use is okay, as is the admissions charge. (The Copyright Act permits copyright owners to object to such charges, but the objection must be served at least one week in advance.)

69

70

71 What is the cost (tuition, room, and board) of a three-year law degree from a prestigious private law school?

(A) $60,000

(B) $120,000

(C) $180,000

(D) $300,000

72 The 1998 Fairness in Music Licensing Act permits TVs to have screens of up to what diagonal measurement without running afoul of public-performance rights?

(A) 29 inches

(B) 55 inches

(C) 0.01 nautical miles

(D) The whole 9 yards

73 In 2006, Utah passed a law requiring death certificates to be signed by whom?

(A) A funeral director

(B) A state or county medical examiner

(C) A member of the clergy

(D) The deceased's eldest blood relative or spouse

74 A writ of "habeas corpus" requires one to

(A) Lose weight

(B) Exhume a body

(C) Produce a prisoner

(D) Join the Marines

71 ⓒ

72 Ⓑ

73 Ⓐ

74 ⓒ

75 Phase II clinical trials generally involve

- (A) A jury of one's peers
- (B) Laboratory rats
- (C) Clinical efficacy studies
- (D) Human-safety studies
- (E) Moot court appellate arguments

76 What is a "Green Card"?

- (A) A certificate of compliance from the U.S. Environmental Protection Agency
- (B) A soccer penalty for severe infraction that requires ejection *and* fines
- (C) U.S. Food and Drug Administration approval of a medical device
- (D) Permission for a noncitizen to reside in the U.S.

77 When Title 27 of the U.S. Code requires "a record of the ballings of the wort," which of the following is it regulating?

- (A) Beer production
- (B) Prostitution in Nevada
- (C) Dermatology statistics
- (D) None of the above

78 A law review article about "dilution" is most likely about which of the following?

- (A) Minimizing inheritance taxes
- (B) Regulating alcohol content
- (C) Protecting trademarks
- (D) Using eye-pupil size as evidence in drunk-driving cases

75 C

76 D

77 A (The statute is directed at brewers.)

78 C (*Dilution* refers to blurring or tarnishing a trademark.)

79 **Hypothetical:**

A woman shopping at a local supermarket slips on a pool of spilled soda and injures her hip, causing pain and requiring medical treatment. The drink was spilled by a ten-year-old playing hooky from school. The school secretary had failed to check the attendance sheets that day, so she hadn't known to notify the boy's parents of his absence. (She had mishandled attendance on prior occasions.) Several shoppers had earlier reported the spill to the manager, who had instructed one of his clerks to clean it up. Because of a hearing problem, the clerk had not heard this order.

The woman's aggressive lawyer sues the store and its manager for her pain and suffering, the school for failing to report the student's absence, the school secretary for negligence, the boy for deliberately creating a dangerous condition, the parents for inadequate supervision, the soda bottler for not using childproof caps, the flooring manufacturer for not using more slip-resistant vinyl, the maker of her shoes for not using more slip-resistant bottoms, and the clerk for failing to obey orders. Will she win?

79 The injured shopper will win against the store and the student. She might win against the boy's parents if she can prove the child acted willfully or maliciously, though many states cap parental liability for their children's torts.

80 The following drawing is from U.S. Patent No. 7,073,223, issued July 11, 2006. What does it illustrate?

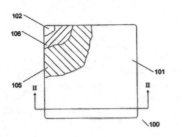

(A) An arrangement of stairs that enables an individual to enter a swimming pool from the front or the side in a manner that minimizes the effects of cold temperatures

(B) An imbedded building cornice that enables the structure to withstand high impacts

(C) A sandbox that allows safe play among children of different ages and sizes

(D) A fart cushion

81 What penalty do consumers risk for removing a "Do Not Remove" tag from a pillow or mattress?

(A) Up to five years in prison and/or a fine of up to $5,000

(B) One-year suspended sentence and/or a $1,000 fine

(C) A fine of up to $100

(D) None

82 The U.S., with 5 percent of the world's population, has what percentage of the world's prison population?

(A) 1%

(B) 10%

(C) 25%

(D) 50%

ANSWERS

 80 (D) (The invention is a "flatulence filter seat cushion for absorbing odor and providing sound attenuation from an anal discharge of a seated individual.")

 81 (D) (The rule applies to employees of the store selling the item.)

 82 (C)

58 STUMP YOUR LAWYER !

83 What is the meaning of the phrase *"nunc pro tunc"*?

   Ⓐ Professionals must perform to a higher standard

   Ⓑ Something happening now should be treated as if it occurred previously

   Ⓒ "A great miracle happened here," a phrase abbreviated on a Chanukah dreidel

   Ⓓ "Now I lay me down to sleep" in Latin

84 What is the meaning of the term *"mutatis mutandis"*?

   Ⓐ Changed as necessary

   Ⓑ Mentally challenged

   Ⓒ Genetic mutations are not patentable

   Ⓓ "Silence turns golden"; technically, a court-ordered prior restraint

85 Many states recognize a "right of publicity" that survives the death of an individual. Match the state on the left with the duration in years of the statutory post-death publicity right on the right:

   Ⓐ California   ① 0

   Ⓑ Florida   ② 40

   Ⓒ Illinois   ③ 50

   Ⓓ Indiana   ④ 70

   Ⓔ New York   ⑤ 100

ANSWERS

83 B

84 A

85 A 4
    B 2
    C 3
    D 5
    E 1

86 How long after a person's death does the right of publicity survive in Tennessee, Elvis Presley's home state?

(A) 0 years

(B) 10 years (but continues perpetually if continuously exploited)

(C) 50 years

(D) 100 years

(E) It's perpetual

87 Hypothetical:

An injured person is seeking trial counsel. A law firm offers to handle the matter using a team of three lawyers consisting of a partner whose rate is $375 per hour, a senior associate whose rate is $275 per hour, and a junior associate who bills at $225 per hour. The firm proposes to use a "blended rate" of $285 per hour for services performed by any of them and agrees to cap its fees at $75,000.

Which of the following is likely to occur?

(A) The partner will push as much work as possible down to the most junior associates

(B) The senior associate will effectively be in charge, unless the senior partner is *really* interested in the client or the dispute

(C) The bookkeeping department will make at least one billing error before it gets the bills right for this client

(D) At some point, the law firm will identify certain services as outside the scope of the project and therefore not subject to the cap

86 Ⓑ

87 All of the above. Each is likely to occur at some point.

88 Suppose Santa Claus informs his U.S. law firm that next December 24, he will leave the North Pole with his reindeer-drawn sleigh full of toys for good little boys and girls. Which of the following can his lawyers ignore?

(A) The U.S. Department of Homeland Security, U.S. Citizenship and Immigration Services

(B) The U.S.–Arctic Tax Treaty

(C) The Public Interest Research Group's annual Survey of Toy Safety

(D) "Importation of Pets, Other Animals, and Animal Products into the United States," Centers for Disease Control and Prevention, National Center for Infectious Diseases, Division of Global Migration and Quarantine

89 In 2006, Las Vegas passed an ordinance, possibly the first in the nation, prohibiting people from doing what in local parks?

(A) Sheltering the homeless

(B) Smiting the wicked

(C) Feeding the poor

(D) Clothing the naked

(E) Getting naked

90 This former Lincoln cabinet member and Supreme Court Justice presided over the impeachment of Andrew Johnson. He is

(A) Marlin P. Chase

(B) Halibut P. Chase

(C) Salmon P. Chase

(D) Kingfish P. Chase

88 Ⓑ

89 Ⓒ

90 Ⓒ

91 **Hypothetical:**

A behavioral engineer has an idea for a new concept restaurant that solves the problem of diners who can't decide what to order. When making reservations online, diners complete a thirty-question profile sheet that reveals their preferences regarding food, decor, lighting, and service. When they arrive at the restaurant, they are greeted at the door by name and served meals that have been selected scientifically, using techniques developed by the engineer, to match the diners' food preferences. The engineer calls this system "Prefab Dining" and would like to trademark that term.

Which of the following statements are true?

(A) If this method of matching customer likes with food choices hasn't already been patented or publicly used, the engineer can patent it

(B) The engineer's list of questions may be copyrightable

(C) If the term "Prefab Dining" has already been used, either as a mark or as a generic reference to food services, it probably can't be trademarked

(D) The engineer's waitresses can wear skimpy black tops and athletic shorts without infringing the trade dress of a well-known national chain

(E) All of the above

92 **Of the following, who is not a lawyer?**

(A) Julio Iglesias

(B) John Cleese

(C) Geraldo Rivera

(D) William Shatner

(E) Howard Cosell

91

92 Ⓓ (though not all the others practiced law)

93 **A copyright lasts**

(A) For the author's life

(B) For the life of the author plus seventy years

(C) For twenty years after registration with the Copyright Office

(D) Until the author's heirs file a certificate dedicating the work to the public domain with the Office of Copyright Divestiture

(E) As long as Disney wants

94 **A "submarine patent" is**

(A) A patent that costs more than it earns for the inventor

(B) A patent whose issuance is deliberately delayed by the inventor

(C) Protection for an invention related to a sandwich

(D) A glossy shoe worn in the Navy

95 **Identify *each* of the following that a prospective employer should *not* ask a job applicant:**

(A) Do you plan to get pregnant?

(B) Have you performed a similar job before?

(C) Have you always been this obese?

(D) Were you bar mitzvahed?

96 **How much wood could a woodchuck collect if a woodchuck were camping at Washington's Lake Chelan National Recreation Area?**

(A) All trees found within forest fuel-reduction areas produced by manual thinning

(B) Snags within 200 feet of primary roads within fuel-reduction areas felled by park personnel

(C) Hazardous floating logs removed and stockpiled by the Park Service

(D) All of the above

(E) No firewood gathering is permitted

93   Ⓑ

94   Ⓑ

95   Ⓐ Ⓒ and Ⓓ

96   Ⓓ

97 How many patents have been issued by the U.S. Patent and Trademark Office since its creation in the 18th century?

(A) 150,000

(B) 1 million

(C) 7 million

(D) 70 million

98 A "codicil" is

(A) An amendment to a bill by voice vote

(B) A fish the law deems too small to be removed from the ocean

(C) A modification to a will

(D) A cold remedy

99 The "Rule Against Perpetuities" prohibits which of the following?

(A) Federal judges sitting on the bench after age eighty-four

(B) The chartering of a national bank for more than twenty years

(C) Insurance companies selling annuities to felons

(D) The creation of contingent interests that may not vest within twenty-one years after any life in being at the time of their creation

100 U.S. beer-labeling requirements mandate a government warning concerning pregnant women and operating machinery. What is the minimum print size per character on a 12-ounce bottle?

(A) 2 millimeters

(B) 4 millimeters

(C) 6 millimeters

(D) The government doesn't waste taxpayer dollars regulating font size

97 C

98 C

99 D

100 A (2 millimeters high per character, up to 25 characters per inch)

101 At common law, an illegal lottery (or gamble) contains three features:

(A) Price, prize, and chance

(B) Price, fraud, and horse racing

(C) Price, prize, and Publishers Clearing House

(D) Price, prize, and rules in tiny print (up to 25 characters per inch)

102 Under the Federal Trade Commission "Made in the USA" Standard, which of the following must be labeled to disclose its U.S. content?

(A) Textile, wool, and fur products

(B) Computer chips

(C) Cattle

(D) All of the above

(E) None of the above

103 The New Hampshire General Court (the state legislature) has how many legislators?

(A) 24

(B) 112

(C) 264

(D) 424

104 The term "laches" refers to which of the following?

(A) Old men who date young women

(B) Prejudicial delay in bringing a claim

(C) Young children left without parental guidance

(D) Chanukah pancakes

101 Ⓐ

102 Ⓐ

103 Ⓓ

104 Ⓑ

105 The following is a bust of whom?

(A) Solon, Athenian lawmaker

(B) Solomon, author of first published judicial decision

(C) Suleiman, Giver of Laws

(D) Slobodan, accused war criminal

106 Which of the following poets was *not* a lawyer?

(A) James Russell Lowell

(B) Edgar Lee Masters

(C) William Carlos Williams

(D) Wallace Stevens

(E) Archibald MacLeish

107 True or False?

In the eyes of the law, both deodorants and antiperspirants are subject to the low-level labeling requirements for cosmetics.

108 "Equitable servitude" refers to

(A) Duties imposed on officers of the law

(B) Liens placed on transferred property

(C) Marriage

(D) Proposed alternative to the Emancipation Proclamation establishing "separate but equal" plantations

105 Ⓐ

106 Ⓒ

107 False (Because antiperspirants affect bodily functions, they must be labeled as drugs.)

108 Ⓑ

109 The term "remittitur" refers to

(A) An order to resubmit court papers

(B) A reduction in a will bequest to benefit a disinherited spouse or child

(C) A court-ordered decrease of an excessive jury award

(D) Gloving both hands of a convicted batterer

110 Of the following contemporary thriller writers, who is *not* a lawyer?

(A) Scott Turow

(B) John Grisham

(C) Richard North Patterson

(D) James Patterson

(E) Lisa Scottoline

111 Adultery and fornication both involve sex out of wedlock. What's the difference?

(A) In adultery, at least one partner is twenty-one or older

(B) In adultery, at least one partner is married to someone else

(C) In fornication, at least one partner is a farm animal

(D) There is no difference

112 Legal issues in the publishing industry caused by "orphan works" involve

(A) A parentless waif, such as Little Orphan Annie

(B) Out-of-print books

(C) Rarely cited or quoted articles

(D) Authors who can't be located

109   C

110   D

111   B

112   D

113 Under California law, which of the following offenses carries the greatest penalties?

(A) Littering

(B) Urinating in public

(C) Injuring police dogs

(D) Possessing up to 28.5 grams of marijuana

114 The City Code of Little Rock, Arkansas prohibits doing what at a sandwich shop open after 9 P.M.?

(A) Honking a horn

(B) Removing your shoes

(C) Removing other diners' shoes

(D) Failing to tip servers

(E) Stem cell research

115 In 2006, the Massachusetts Supreme Judicial Court became the first major court to deny tobacco companies the ability to defend personal-injury lawsuits by arguing that

(A) Tobacco has important benefits, like giving people with *truly awful* breath just plain bad breath

(B) Smoking tobacco is, like riding a motorcycle without a helmet, a fundamental right of a free people guaranteed by the U.S. Constitution

(C) The tobacco industry pays billions in taxes to federal and state government and, directly or indirectly, employs hundreds of thousands of people

(D) Smokers know the health risks of smoking and thus are responsible for hurting themselves

113 C

114 A

115 D

116 What do you call a clause in a contract that limits the period of time during which one party can sue the other for breach?

(A) A force majeure clause

(B) A private statute of limitations

(C) A "hell or high water" clause

(D) A "no huddle offense" clause

117 How many Titles are there in the U.S. Code?

(A) 25

(B) 50

(C) 100

(D) 500

118 Identify the number and subject of the last Chapter of the Internal Revenue Code.

(A) 25, Alcohol, Tobacco, and Certain Other Excise Taxes

(B) 35, Taxes on Wagering

(C) 100, Group Health Plan Requirements

(D) 500, Underused Loopholes

116 (B)

117 (B)

118 (C)

119 Hypothetical:

Joe, an employee at will, cuts work—claiming illness—to attend a Red Sox–Yankees game. Entering Fenway Park, he encounters David Ortiz and, while getting Big Papi's autograph, is caught on film by a local photographer. The photo, which displays a prominent, beaming Joe and a barely visible Ortiz, appears the next day on the front page of the local newspaper's sports section. Joe's boss, a Yankees fan, fires Joe for skipping work. Whom can Joe sue?

Suppose that a year after the above firing, the photo of Joe appears in an advertisement for Major League Baseball. Joe is still an employee at will and his new boss, another ardent Yankees fan, sees the ad and fires Joe on the spot. Now whom can Joe sue?

120 What is a 510(k)?

- (A) Type of pension account
- (B) Average amount of a small claims court award in Texas
- (C) SEC rule permitting sale of securities without registration
- (D) Abbreviated FDA approval process

121 Under the Constitution, one must be how old and a citizen for how long to run for the U.S. Senate?

122 Under the Constitution, one must be how old and a citizen for how long to run for the House of Representatives?

123 Under the Constitution, in addition to Presidential nomination and Senate approval, what requirements must one satisfy to serve on the Supreme Court?

119 The first time around Joe can't sue anyone. The second time, he might have a claim against Major League Baseball for violating his publicity rights, but he still can't sue his employer.

120

121 Thirty years old, nine years a citizen

122 Twenty-five years old, seven years a citizen

123 None

124 Who wrote *The Federalist Papers*, which supported adoption of the U.S. Constitution?

(A) Alexander Hamilton

(B) John Jay

(C) James Madison

(D) All of the above

(E) None of the above

125 The CAN-SPAM Act did which of the following?

(A) Granted Hormel's Spam trademark similar protection to that given the Olympic Rings and Red Cross

(B) Regulated the subject lines of interstate e-mails

(C) Regulated the interstate sale of canned meat by-products

(D) Regulated electronic communications about Canadian girlfriends

126 In intellectual property law, what are "mask works"?

(A) Costumes and similar functional items

(B) Aboriginal works of native art

(C) Designs of semiconductor chips

(D) Works registered with the Copyright Office in redacted form to hide trade secrets

124   Ⓓ

125   Ⓑ

126   Ⓒ

127 Hypothetical:

Ellen is about to lose her apartment. A neighbor says he has an empty floor in his house that she can rent for two years for $750 a month, well below fair market rent. Ellen gives the neighbor a $750 down payment, but when she shows up with her belongings two days later, he says he changed his mind and offers to return the money. Ellen says she wants the room.

(A) Can Ellen sue for breach?

(B) Would it matter if the neighbor knew that Ellen's infirm mother lived with her?

(C) Suppose that when the neighbor first took the money, he and Ellen signed a memo stating that he was renting her his third floor for twenty-four months at a rate of $750 per month: Would that affect Ellen's legal rights?

128 What is the maximum dollar amount one can seek in small claims court in Rhode Island?

(A) $1,500

(B) $3,000

(C) $5,000

(D) $10,000

129 What is the maximum dollar amount one can seek in small claims court in New Mexico?

(A) $1,500

(B) $3,000

(C) $5,000

(D) $10,000

127  Regardless of whether Ellen has a dependent mother, few courts would enforce a two-year oral lease. However—older lawyers take note—most states now recognize oral residential leases, for anywhere from one month to a year, so many courts would recognize Ellen's rights for a shorter term.

 With a signed writing, Ellen can sue for the apartment and damages.

128

129

130 Who said, "The law is a ass"?

  (A) Mike Myers (as Shrek)

  (B) Yogi Berra

  (C) Charles Dickens

  (D) William Shakespeare (rebutting Francis Bacon's essay, "The Law is a Elbow")

  (E) Apuleius

131 How does a "Miranda warning" begin?

  (A) With a Mutt and Jeff routine by the police

  (B) "Drop that gun, and come out with your hands up!"

  (C) "Put your right foot in, put your right foot out."

  (D) "You have the right to remain silent."

132 What happened to Ernesto Miranda, after whom the Miranda warning was named?

  (A) Died in prison

  (B) Became a social worker

  (C) Died in a bar fight

  (D) Had a moon of Uranus named after him

133 The following are photographs of whom?

  (A) Wyatt Earp and Doc Holliday

  (B) Joe and Dom DiMaggio

  (C) Janus (front and back view)

  (D) Sacco and Vanzetti

  (E) The Olsen twins

130 Ⓒ

131 Ⓓ

132 Ⓒ

133 Ⓓ

134 **True or False?**

In a 2006 lawsuit in the United Kingdom, Dan Brown's *The Da Vinci Code* was held to infringe the 1982 nonfiction work *Holy Blood, Holy Grail*.

135 **True or False?**

If challenged in court, most Internet gripe sites (for example, IBMsucks.com) are found to infringe the target's (IBM's) brand.

136 **The difference at law between an "affray" and a "riot" is that riots involve**

(A) Destruction of property

(B) Some measure of humor, such as a person slipping on a banana peel

(C) Three or more (in some states, ten or more) people

(D) Weaponry

137 **How many states have shield laws that enable reporters to protect their confidential sources?**

(A) 10–20

(B) 21–30

(C) 31–40

(D) over 40

134   False

135   False

136   Ⓒ

137   Ⓒ   (31 states plus the District of Columbia)

138 Hypothetical:

Carl, a reporter, is told by a source that Dick, the president of a local corporation, has been cooking the books and bilking his workers and the public. Carl doesn't know that his source used to work for Dick, Dick fired him, and these accusations are fabricated. Carl, however, doesn't take the time to check the source's background or seek confirmation because he's in a hurry and worried another reporter might scoop him.

 If Carl's newspaper publishes these false accusations, whom can Dick sue?

 Is Dick's claim as strong if he's a former, high-ranking elected official who was recently in the news because of a highly publicized battle with the city over allegations of fraud?

 If Dick wants to learn the source's identity in order to sue him, can Dick force Carl and his paper to disclose this?

139 If a man brings his foreign-born, non-citizen significant other into the U.S. on a fiancée visa (K-1), how much time does he have before he is required to marry her?

(A) Ninety days
(B) Six months
(C) One year
(D) Three years

140 After an American citizen marries a non-citizen, what's the minimum period the new spouse has to wait to become a naturalized U.S. citizen?

(A) Six months
(B) One year
(C) Three years
(D) Six years

138

A Dick can sue Carl, the paper, and their source for defamation, since Carl and the paper were negligent and the source outright lied.

B If Dick is a former high-level official and still in the news, he is a "public figure" who would need to prove Carl's and the paper's "actual malice" (awareness of falsity or reckless disregard of the truth) to win against them. This doesn't seem the case here, so Dick should lose. But his case remains strong against the source.

C Dick would not get a court to order disclosure if he's in one of the more than 30 states that shield reporters. Even in states without shield laws, Dick may never discover the identity of the real libeler if the reporter refuses to obey a court order to disclose (even after being sent to jail for contempt of court).

139 Ⓐ

140 Ⓒ

141 To call someone "non compos mentis" is to say the person is

(A) Too decomposed to autopsy

(B) Bewitched, bothered, and bewildered

(C) Not the composer he thinks he is

(D) Not fit to fertilize a garden

142 Since 1988, the federal government has tried 124 federal death penalty cases involving 191 defendants. How many executions have resulted?

(A) 0

(B) 3

(C) 13

(D) 30

(E) 126

143 In round numbers, how many plant and animal species are on the Threatened or Endangered Species List in North Dakota?

(A) 10

(B) 100

(C) 300

(D) 500

144 How many Threatened or Endangered Species are there in California?

(A) 10

(B) 100

(C) 300

(D) 500

145 What state has the most Threatened or Endangered Species?

141 (Literally, it means "not of sound mind.")

142 Ⓑ (as of February 2007)

143

144 Ⓒ

145 Hawaii (with 317)

146 Which corporation received the most patents in both 2004 and 2005?

(A) Intel

(B) Toshiba

(C) IBM

(D) Microsoft

(E) Wal-Mart

147 In 2002, Stephen D. Brown patented a novel method of using

(A) Computer storage devices

(B) Soldering irons

(C) Bread crusts

(D) Yo-yos

148 In 1999, Len Kretchman and David Geske patented

(A) A computer storage device

(B) A new type of frisbee

(C) A peanut-butter-and-jelly sandwich

(D) A graphical user interface for a geospatial modulator deployed in automobiles

149 The words *aspirin*, *escalator*, and *cellophane* are examples of trademarks that became

(A) Generic

(B) Descriptive

(C) Diluted

(D) Assigned in gross

(IBM with 3,248 patents in 2004 and 2,941 in 2005)

 (Brown designs yo-yos for Duncan.)

 (They patented a crustless PB&J sandwich.)

150 **Hypothetical:**

Sarah deposits $2,000 in an account at the local branch of a major national bank. She gets a Visa-branded debit card, then takes off with her boyfriend on a major trip across the U.S. In a small town in Idaho her wallet is stolen. When she discovers the theft the next day she immediately contacts the bank. They call her back a day later to say that they're sorry, but whoever stole her wallet immediately used her card to make several major purchases and zeroed out her account. "Nothing we can do," says the bank. "You're out the $2,000." Is she?

151 What blood alcohol level constitutes driving under the influence (DUI) for drivers over 21?

(A) 0.02

(B) 0.08

(C) 0.1

(D) 0.5

(E) 1.0

152 What blood alcohol level constitutes DUI for drivers under 21 in New York, Montana, and Massachusetts?

(A) 0.001

(B) 0.005

(C) 0.01

(D) 0.02

(E) 0.08

No. As long as she properly reported the theft, federal and state laws and banking rules limit her loss to $50.

151 Ⓑ

152 Ⓓ

153 How many marijuana arrests occurred in the U.S. from 1995 to 2005?

- (A) 250,000
- (B) 500,000
- (C) 2.5 million
- (D) 7 million

154 How many Americans admit to having tried marijuana?

- (A) 2.5 million
- (B) 7 million
- (C) 50 million
- (D) 100 million

155 True or False?

Sheila, a forklift operator, complains to her boss about gender discrimination. She's promptly transferred to a less desirable position, though one with the same pay and benefits. She can recover damages under the Equal Employment Opportunity Act as a victim of retaliation.

156 What is the title of the following 18th-century painting?

- (A) *Death of Socrates* (after conviction for corrupting youth)
- (B) *We're No. 1* (Socrates celebrates Athens's victory over Sparta in the Peloponnesian Cup)
- (C) *Socrates Refutes Spouse* (depicted after Mrs. Socrates exited the room)
- (D) *30 Lbs. in 30 Days!* (Socrates extols the lo-carb diet)

153 Ⓓ

154 Ⓓ

155 True

156 Ⓐ

157 What did British philosopher Thomas Hobbes describe as "nasty, brutish, and short"?

(A) The Code of Hammurabi

(B) His career with Manchester United

(C) Life in a state of nature, before government and the rule of law

(D) Mrs. Hobbes

158 Match the famous person on the left with the area of law he or she has influenced the most.

(A) Sonny Bono   (1) Laws of inheritance

(B) Vanna White   (2) Copyright law

(C) Paul Anka   (3) Tax law

(D) Anna Nicole Smith   (4) Securities law

(E) Al Capone   (5) Right of publicity

159 The FDA process for approving pharmaceuticals focuses primarily on

(A) Cost and safety

(B) Cost and efficacy

(C) Safety and efficacy

(D) Pill color and catchy name

160 The pharmaceutical patent for which product expired in 2006, thereby undermining a $4–5 billion market for its producer?

(A) Lipitor

(B) Gondor

(C) Zocor

(D) Boromir

(E) Sildenafil

157 Ⓒ

158
Ⓐ	②
Ⓑ	⑤
Ⓒ	④
Ⓓ	①
Ⓔ	③

159 Ⓒ (but don't assume they're not interested in color and branding)

160 Ⓒ (Lipitor was challenged but survives, and earns twice what Zocor made.)

161 The Scopes Monkey Trial concerned what?

- (A) A Tennessee high school teacher discussing evolution
- (B) Procter & Gamble's use of orangutans in clinical mouthwash trials
- (C) Bushnell's use of chimpanzees to test the accuracy of rifle sights
- (D) A University of Georgia professor falsifying research evidence

162 What movie was based on the Scopes Monkey Trial?

- (A) *George of the Jungle*
- (B) *12 Angry Men*
- (C) *A Mighty Wind*
- (D) *Inherit the Wind*

163 In addition to speech, the First Amendment protects which of the following?

- (A) Religion, the press, the right to bear arms, and the right to assemble
- (B) The press, the right to bear arms, religion, and equal access to law
- (C) The press, petitioning, picketing, and proselytizing
- (D) Truth, justice, and the American way

164 This 19th-century engraving depicts what?

- (A) William Seward's Poker Club
- (B) Waiting Room, Springfield Maternity Ward, 1854
- (C) *Abe and the Log Cabin Boys* album cover (1863)
- (D) The first reading of the Emancipation Proclamation before the Cabinet

161 (A)

162 (D)

163 (C)

164 (D)

165 Hypothetical:

Tom lived in an apartment with his collie. This violated his lease, which prohibited pets; but since the dog appeared harmless, the landlord looked the other way. In January the collie bit Alice, a first. This surprised Tom, who kept the news from the landlord. In February the collie attacked Betty. The landlord learned about it and insisted Tom get rid of the dog. Tom agreed but did nothing. Neither did the landlord. Finally, in March the collie broke the leash keeping her in the apartment and attacked Charlie, the mailman. Who can Alice, Betty, and Charlie sue?

166 How many states have laws that prohibit or regulate the keeping of wild or exotic animals?

(A) Fewer than 10
(B) 10–30
(C) 31–44
(D) All 50

167 According to a famous saying attributed to Otto von Bismarck, what two things do you not want to see made?

(A) Laws and egg salad
(D) Laws and sausage
(C) Laws and lutefisk with *schweinsmagen* wrapped in head cheese
(D) Heads wrapped in lutefisk with *schweinsmagen* and egg salad

Alice probably has no claim. In most locales, every dog still has a free bite. Betty can sue Tom but not the landlord, who didn't know the dog was vicious. Charlie can sue Tom, probably the landlord, and possibly the maker and seller of the leash.

 (35 states)

167 Ⓑ

168 Hypothetical:

While Debbie and Cyndi were walking together, a passing car sideswiped a garbage can, knocking it toward them. The garbage can should have been removed by the owner of the house a day earlier, per town ordinance. Cyndi leaped out of the way, spraining her ankle, while Debbie jumped into the street, getting hit by a second car speeding by. Steve, a doctor golfing nearby, came over to help Debbie, but misdiagnosed her injury—a silly mistake—which worsened her condition and prolonged her recovery. What claims does each woman have, and what can she recover? Does it matter if Steve, the doctor, sends Debbie a bill?

169 In New York City, how many adult passengers are permitted in a yellow sedan taxicab in addition to the driver?

(A) 3

(B) 4

(C) 5

(D) No limit

170 Are any additional passengers allowed into a New York City taxi beyond the above number?

(A) Yes, one passenger under the age of three, if using a child seat

(B) Yes, one passenger under the age of five, provided his or her buttocks rest on the seat and a seat belt is worn

(C) Yes, one passenger under age seven, if held on a lap

(D) No

168 Cyndi can sue the driver of the first car and possibly the homeowner. Debbie can sue both, plus the driver of the speeding second car. Steve, the physician, is protected by Good Samaritan laws unless he misdiagnosed willfully (or, in many places, grossly negligently). However, since most Good Samaritan laws apply only to help rendered without expectation of payment, sending a bill may subject Steve to liability for malpractice.

169

170

171 What is an "integration" clause?

(A) A government-contract clause requiring equal access among races and religions

(B) A statutory provision requiring government bids to be open to all

(C) A court's determination that a plaintiff's claim for separate damages from multiple wrongs reflects one injury and must be combined

(D) A clause stating that a contract is the complete expression of the parties' agreement

172 True or False?

In a 2006 lawsuit in the United Kingdom, the Beatles' Apple Records, which uses a logo with a Granny Smith apple, won a lawsuit to prevent Apple Computer from using its own Apple logo for its iTunes Music Store.

173 Under federal automobile regulations, to prevent damage to the car body and safety equipment, passenger-car bumpers must be able to withstand impacts at what speed?

(A) 2.5 miles per hour

(B) 10 mph

(C) 25 mph

(D) 50 mph

171 Ⓓ

172 False

173 Ⓐ

174 Hypothetical:

Bill, who sells software, learns that his best customer just signed a contract to purchase a suite of add-on programs from Bill's major competitor. Bill calls the customer's vice president of procurement and claims he's heard many serious complaints about the competitor's products. This is a lie. Bill also warns that if the customer doesn't cancel its contract with the competitor, Bill won't sell them his company's newest operating system for at least a year. Since the customer needs that new operating system more than it needs the competitor's add-ons, it cancels its order with the competitor, thereby breaching the contract.

What claims, if any, can the competitor make against the customer, Bill, and his company?

175 In most cases, who has a right to exercise the "marital privilege," which prevents one spouse from being forced to testify against the other spouse in criminal proceedings?

(A) A presently married spouse against whom the other would testify

(B) A presently married spouse who would give testimony

(C) A presently or previously married spouse against whom witness would testify

(D) A presently or previously married spouse who would give testimony

176 Which of the following are elements of common-law burglary?

(A) Breaking and entering

(B) Dwelling

(C) Nighttime

(D) Felonious intent

(E) Possessing a weapon

The competitor can sue the customer for breach of contract and Bill and his company for defamation, unfair competition, and intentional interference with contract. If Bill's company is a monopoly, it may have violated antitrust laws as well.

176 (A) (B) (C) and (D)

177 Which Supreme Court Justice famously wrote, "I know it when I see it," and what is the "it"?

(A) Scalia, an obscene gesture

(B) Powell, seborrheic dermatitis

(C) Rehnquist, lutefisk with *schweinsmagen*

(D) Ginsburg, the perfect fur coat to dress up a jeans ensemble

(E) Stewart, obscenity

178 Alabama law 13A-14-4 punishes by a $500 fine and/or one year in jail doing what in public?

(A) Dancing

(B) Urinating

(C) Impersonating clergy

(D) Unleashing a dog with a "propensity to bite"

(E) Singing "Sweet Home Alabama" off-key

179 Hypothetical:

Imelda sells shoes for a small local store. She is paid for a 40-hour week but is expected to work more, without overtime pay, if she's needed. After she works a grueling 60-hour week, a friend tells her she's due overtime pay by law. Imelda asks the company treasurer about overtime and gets fired on the spot. Two weeks later, her company files for bankruptcy, just after the president and the treasurer have paid themselves whopping bonuses. Can Imelda sue her company, or anyone else, for the overtime pay she never received? Would it matter if she'd agreed in writing that only her first 40 hours of work in any week would count as work time?

177

178

179 Imelda is entitled to overtime, at least time and a half her regular rate. She can't waive this, despite her agreement. She may even be owed extra damages because she was fired for asserting her rights. Imelda can sue the company and the officers, who may be personally liable for their company's failure to pay the wages owed her.

180 In *Brandenburg v. Ohio*, the Supreme Court acknowledged that it does not violate the Constitution to prohibit an individual from doing what in a movie theater?

(A) Shouting out the movie's ending

(B) Saving seats for more than one friend

(C) Falsely shouting "Fire!"

(D) Under cover of darkness, eating a neighbor's popcorn

181 Executive Order 11246 concerned

(A) Equal employment opportunity

(B) The death of John Wilkes Booth by lethal injection

(C) Dry cleaning a blue dress belonging to an M. Lewinsky

(D) Establishing the tarantula hawk wasp as the official insect of New Mexico

182 The Senate has sat as a court of impeachment in the case of which federal official named Nixon?

(A) Richard Nixon

(B) Jay Nixon

(C) Trot Nixon

(D) Walter Nixon

183 What is the cost of software piracy worldwide?

(A) $100–$200 million

(B) $500–$750 million

(C) $1–$3 billion

(D) $30–$40 billion

180 C

181 A (though the tarantula hawk wasp *is* New Mexico's official insect)

182 D (Judge Walter L. Nixon, Jr. was removed from office in 1989; President Nixon was never impeached.)

183 D (According to the Business Software Alliance, piracy cost $32.4 billion in 2004 and $34 billion in 2005.)

184 Compare the piracy rate (percentage counterfeited) for software sold in the U.S. and software sold in China in 2005:

(A) 2% U.S. vs. 29% China

(B) 11% U.S. vs. 68% China

(C) 21% U.S. vs. 84% China

(D) 33% U.S. vs. 96% China

185 What existing law regulates earthly parties' activities in outer space?

(A) The Agreement on the Rescue of Astronauts, the Return of Astronauts, and the Return of Objects Launched into Outer Space

(B) The U.N. Convention on Robots On-Board Biodiverse Inter-planetary Exploratory Vehicles (the so-called ROBBIE Law)

(C) The Treaty on the Quarantine of Interstellar Life-Forms

(D) The federal Alien Tort Claims Act

186 Under federal regulations that require a permit to launch an orbital vehicle, to obtain safety approval an applicant must show that the risk from debris from the applicant's launch to the collective public shall not exceed

(A) 1 casualty per launch

(B) .001 casualty per launch

(C) .00003 casualty per launch

(D) .0000000000003 casualty per launch

(E) There are no such casualty calculations

184 Ⓒ

185 Ⓐ

186 Ⓒ

187 Hypothetical:

Larry and Sergey decide to start a new Internet business. They interest a group of angel investors, who offer to give them $500,000 for 20% of the company, provided they receive *full ratchet protection*, *tagalong rights*, and *registration rights*. What are they asking for?

(A) The angels want rights to buy into later rounds (to keep their ownership at 20%), to invest in the founders' next startup, and to require the filing of patents and trademarks in the company's intellectual property.

(B) The angels want rights to prevent arbitrage, buy debentures, and open offices in foreign jurisdictions.

(C) The angels want the benefit of cheaper prices charged later investors, pro rata inclusion in subsequent rounds, and a right to sell their stock in public markets.

(D) The angels want rights to hire carpenters, be invited to the founders' parties, and be included in the company dental plan.

188 How many H-1B (temporary worker) visas are issued annually by the U.S.?

(A) 65,000

(B) 85,000

(C) 100,000

(D) 185,000

189 In New York City, how deep must one dig a human grave?

(A) Six feet

(B) Four feet (no minimum for a concrete vault)

(C) Three feet (two feet for a concrete vault)

(D) There is no rule

187

188 (though 20,000 are reserved for persons with advanced degrees, so we'll also accept answer (A))

189 Ⓒ

190 Match the law on the left (named after a victim) with the law's purpose on the right.

(A) Megan's Law (California)

(B) Amilia's Law (New Hampshire)

(C) Haley's Law (Tennessee)

(D) Melanie's Law (Massachusetts)

(E) Ashley's Law (Pennsylvania)

(1) Licensing gas and propane handlers

(2) Stiffening penalties for child abusers

(3) Graduating students with disabilities

(4) Publicizing sex offender information

(5) Ignition controls over drunk drivers

191 President Bush has appended a "signing statement" asserting his right to judge the constitutionality of laws passed by Congress—and thus ignore those he judges unconstitutional—to how many bills?

(A) Less than 25

(B) 100–250

(C) 275–500

(D) Over 800

192 In the 2006 U.S. Supreme Court case *Hamdan v. Rumsfeld*, the Court held that the government violated the Geneva Convention regarding a prisoner held at

(A) Andersonville

(B) Guantánamo Bay

(C) Abu Ghraib

(D) A Star Trek convention

(E) Band Camp

190 (A) (4)
     (B) (1)
     (C) (2)
     (D) (5)
     (E) (3)

191 (D)

192 (B)

193 Under the doctrine of "inevitable disclosure," a company can

(A) Enjoin an ex-employee who knows company secrets from working in a position that requires using the secrets

(B) Receive twenty years of patent protection in exchange for disclosing the invention to the world

(C) Exploit a competitor's trade secrets that would otherwise surely be discovered by people working in the field

(D) Seek a court order requiring former employees to disclose work products they created for the company and which are therefore owned by the company

194 Hypothetical:

Alex and John, two programmers, decide to leave their current employer, Acme Software, and start a competing business. Both had signed contracts promising to keep Acme information secret and assigning to Acme any patentable inventions they developed, but neither agreed not to compete. Alex leaves with a CD containing unpatented software code that he wrote (mostly at home) as part of an Acme assignment and promptly replaces the Acme copyright notice on the code with one in his own name. After quitting, John enters Acme's computer network using a "backdoor" he created while he was an employee and downloads several documents containing Acme's confidential marketing plans.

When Alex and John launch their business a month later, using the copied software and the downloaded marketing plan, Acme sues for breach of contract, theft of trade secrets, and an injunction against their competing.

A Will Acme win?

B Has it missed any tricks?

C Have Alex and John done anything criminal?

193

194 A Acme should win for breach of contract and misappropriation, but not to prevent competition. However, if the jurisdiction embraces "inevitable disclosure," the court might prohibit their performing tasks that would exploit their knowledge of Acme's secrets.

B Acme should also sue for copyright infringement, trespass, and violating the Computer Fraud and Abuse Act (CFAA).

C Willfully copying the software and replacing the copyright notice may be criminal copyright infringement; stealing trade secrets is criminal in many states, and could also be a crime under the Economic Espionage Act; and the unauthorized use of the computer is criminal under the CFAA.

195 This Civil War hero taught at Harvard, sat on the Massachusetts Supreme Judicial Court, then served 30 years on the U.S. Supreme Court and helped Franklin Delano Roosevelt choose his successor. Who is he?

(A) Wendell Wilkie

(B) Oliver Wendell Holmes, Sr.

(C) Oliver Wendell Holmes, Jr.

(D) Sherlock "Katie" Holmes

196 Hypothetical:

Rose orders a book from a mail order book club but is surprised to receive two books in the mail. The second book contains a note that says the club is so sure she'll love it that the company decided to send it to her for half price. Rose doesn't want to pay for the book. What will the law allow her to do? In particular, must she either pay for it or return it?

197 In which of the following states can a person become a lawyer without passing a bar examination?

(A) Louisiana

(B) Wisconsin

(C) Idaho and Nebraska

(D) New Hampshire and Vermont

(E) None of them

(195)

(196) Federal law permits recipients of unordered merchandise to treat it as a gift. Rose needn't do anything and can keep the second book.

(197) (New Hampshire is scheduled to join Wisconsin in 2008.)

198 How many states have laws permitting grandparents to petition for visitation rights?

(A) 50

(B) 40

(C) 20

(D) 10

(E) 1

199 Hypothetical:

Jay, an editor at Publishing House X, conceives the idea of a humorous quiz book for lawyers. He asks Howie, a lawyer who writes humor, to author it. Howie likes the idea, tells his priest, Father Shannon (a former lawyer), and agrees with Jay on rights, advances, royalties, and delivery date. Jay promises to send Howie a contract, and Howie starts writing. After a month no contract has arrived. An annoyed Howie proposes the idea to Publisher Y, who loves it and offers a huge advance. Howie accepts, signs a contract, and tells Jay he changed his mind. Meanwhile, Father Shannon sneakily sells the idea to Publisher Z. Father Shannon's book comes out a month before Howie's, *really* hurting sales. Who can sue whom for what? In particular, can Jay sue Howie for stealing the idea? Can Howie sue Father Shannon?

Ⓐ (though many laws are restrictive—for example,
requiring parents to be dead or divorcing)

 Because the book idea is scintillating, insightful, and just
plain hilarious—sure to sell millions of copies—Publisher X
can sue Howie for "idea misappropriation," at least in jurisdictions that recognize this tort.

Regardless of how that claim fares, Howie and Jay made a
contract for Howie to write a book, so Publisher X can also
sue Howie for breach. Unless Publisher Y knew there was a
contract and induced Howie's breach, Publisher X can't sue
Publisher Y. Publisher X's claim against Father Shannon is
also weak.

Howie can sue Father Shannon for abusing their confidential relationship by stealing the idea. But unless Publisher Z
knew about the theft, Howie and Publisher Y probably can't
sue Publisher Z.